Mother, What is the Moon?

妈妈,
月亮是什么?

David Griswold
Eliza Reisfeld

Wendy Briggs and Gorden Wang

ORANGE HOUSE
PUBLISHING©

Library of Congress Cataloging-in-Publication Data
Griswold, David.
I. Reisfeld, Eliza.
Mother, What is the Moon? / David Griswold, Illustrated by Eliza Reisfeld
Translated by Wendy Briggs and Gorden Wang– 1st ed. Mandarin Bilingual

Summary: A mother and son's poetic exploration of why the moon changes shape in the sky.
ISBN-13:978-1503294653

[1. Juvenile Fiction: Nature & the Natural World. 2. Poetry: General. 3. Juvenile Fiction: Bedtime and Dreams]

"Mother?"
　"Yes, dear?"

"妈妈？"
　"嗳，宝贝？"

"What is the moon?"
"月亮是什么？"

The moon my dear,
is *many things.*

噢,月亮啊 , 月亮是变幻之神 .

The moon is a *bright hole* in a thick blue blanket.

夜晚的天空就像是又厚又黑的毯子.这时月亮就是
镶在毯子上的一个闪闪发亮的银盘.

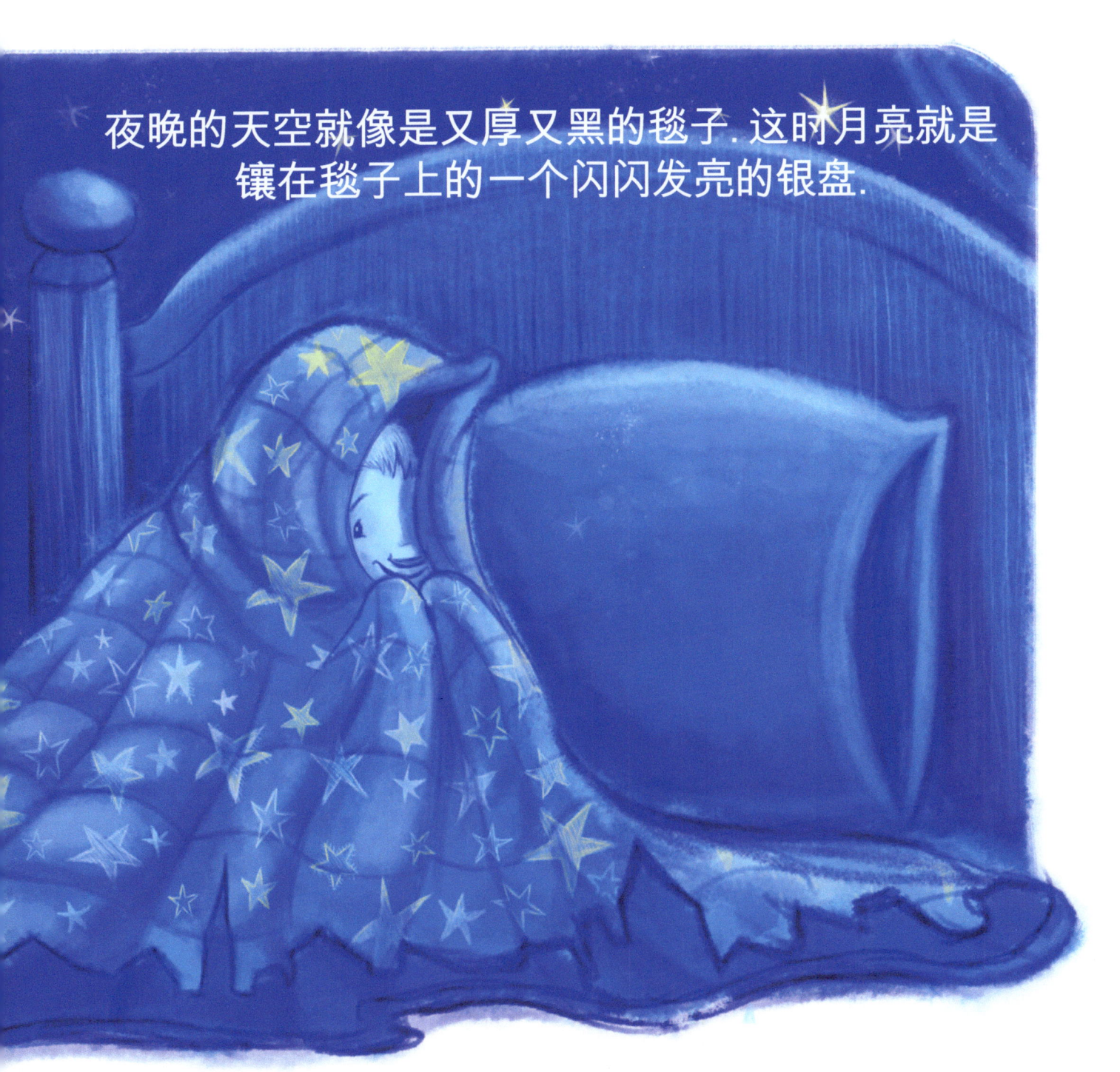

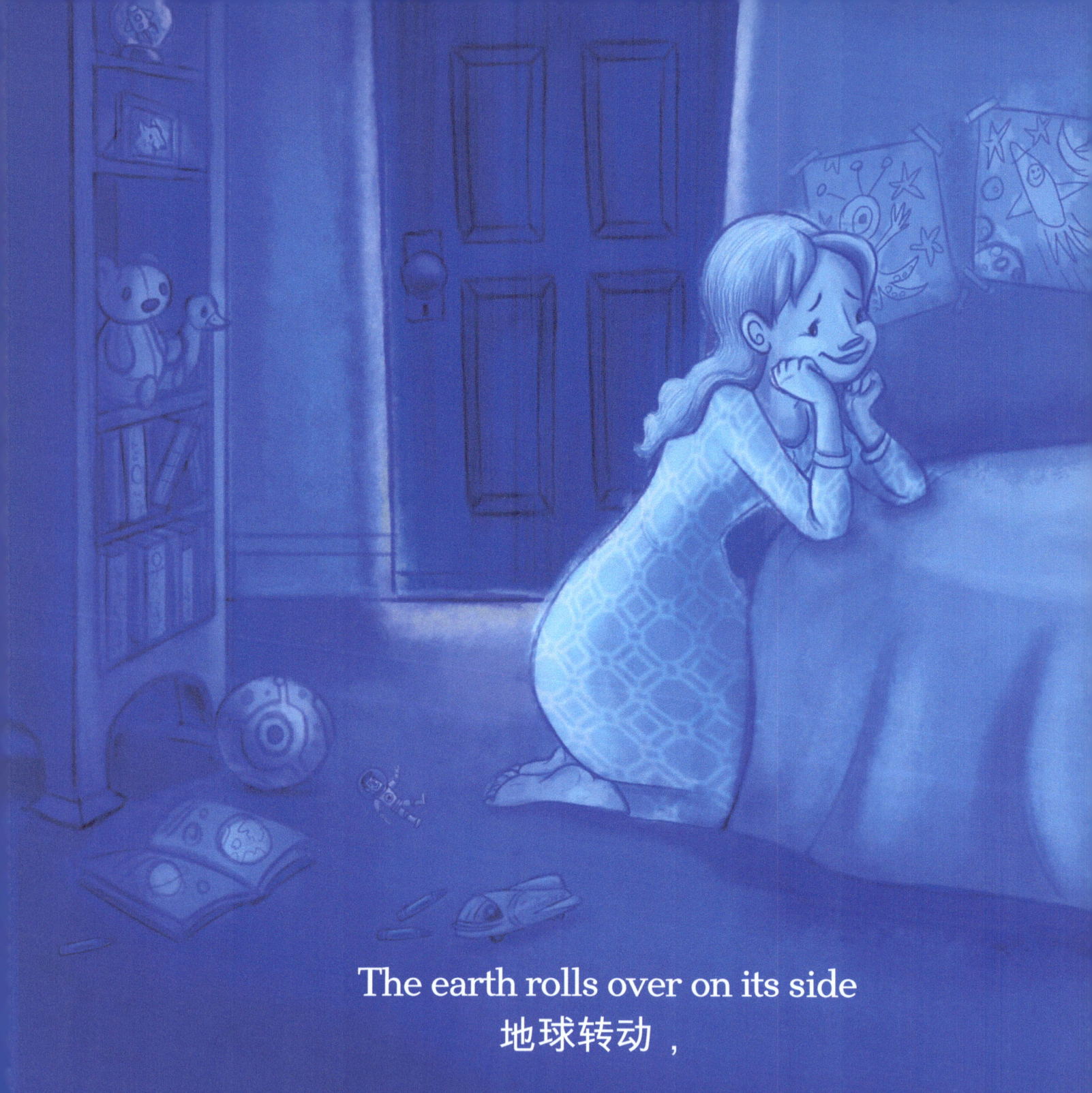

The earth rolls over on its side
地球转动，

and the hole is hidden from view.
银盘会渐渐从我们的眼前消失.

The moon is a *light* looking through a door.

快看！月亮穿过门孔了，她又变成了一束光.

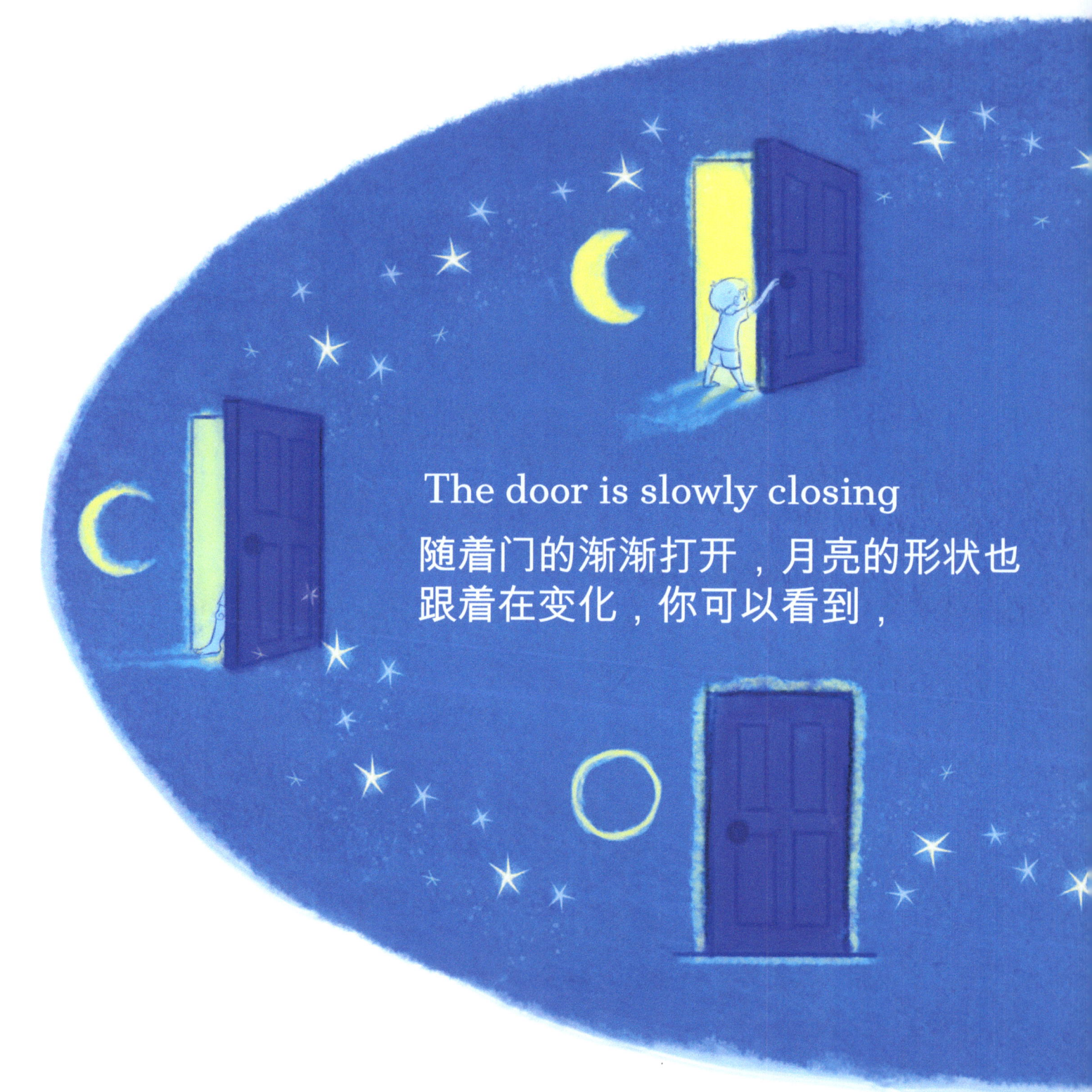

The door is slowly closing

随着门的渐渐打开，月亮的形状也
跟着在变化，你可以看到，

and slowly opening.

先是弯弯的银钩，接着是玉做的
雕弓，再接着是圆圆的明镜.

The moon is a
white stone
in the dark sands of a cool river bed.

月亮还会变成在河床泥沙上的卵石 - -
块圆圆的白玉.

Some nights we see its full circle.
有时候，月亮展现在我们眼前的是一轮满满的圆月；

Other nights

有时候，她却遮上面纱，

we see only

只露出半张笑脸；又有时，

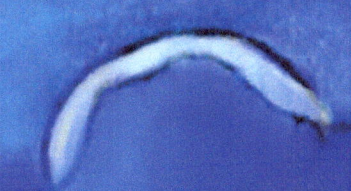

its parts.

她会藏起大半个身影，天空上只挂着一把弯弯的镰刀．

Other nights we see only the dark waters

有时侯，月亮会躲起来，天空就像深深的海水 - -

and the small pebbles
of the the stars.

月亮把天空留给了宝石般闪烁的璀灿的群星.

The moon is a *ball of snow*

月亮还在变，这时又变成了一个雪球．

gathered up from an endless field.

看，这个雪球在那一望无际的雪地上越滚越大.

As it melts, its snowflakes are caught

on the tips of the wheat.

最后，雪球融化了！
化在了麦穗的尖尖上.

The moon is a *smile*

月亮露出了笑脸，

that creates the laughter of the stars.

星星都跟着笑了.

On a night like tonight,

the sky is full of laughter.

有的晚上，就像今天晚上吧，月光明媚，
群星闪耀，一张张笑脸，一阵阵笑声，充
满了整个世界.

The moon my dear,
is *all* these things

宝贝，月亮就是所有这些啊...

and many more...
其实，还远远不止这些.

"Mother?"
    "Yes, dear?"

"妈妈？"
    "嗳，宝贝？"

"What am I?"

"那我是什么？"

You, my dear are the *moon*

that *shines* in my heart.

你，我的宝贝，你就是月亮，就是闪
亮在我心中的月亮.

You my dear,

你，我的宝贝，
你就是变幻之神 - -

are *many things.*

就是我的整个世界.

www.ingramcontent.com/pod-product-compliance
Lightning Source LLC
Chambersburg PA
CBHW060838290526
45792CB00006BB/1981